3AM - Poems and Stories From the Other Mind

Poetic Journeys, Volume 2

Charles Harvey

Published by Wes Writers and Publishers, 2018.

While every precaution has been taken in the preparation of this book, the publisher assumes no responsibility for errors or omissions, or for damages resulting from the use of the information contained herein.

3AM - POEMS AND STORIES FROM THE OTHER MIND

First edition. March 29, 2018.

ISBN: 978-1878774149

Written by Charles Harvey.

Table of Contents

3AM – Poems and Stories From the Other Mind
by
Charles Harvey

* * * * *

PUBLISHED BY:
Wes Writers and Publishers
3AM – Poems and Stories From the Other Mind
Copyright © 2017 by Charles Harvey

Disclaimer

This is a work of fiction. The names, characters, places, and incidents are products of the writer's imagination and are not to be construed as real. Any resemblance to persons, living or dead, actual events, organizations, or locales is entirely coincidental.

A poem comes innocently into the world.

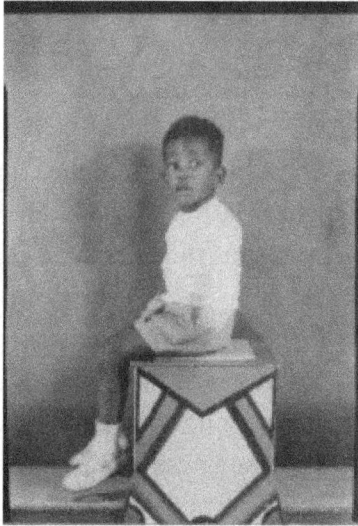

Epigraph

How did it get so late so soon?

Dr. Seuss

IT's3AM

Hunger

Walking through the house naked at 3 a.m.
  The air is your garment
  Used Trojans cushion your feet.
  You hear your roommate making love
  With the one, you called *Dr. Spock* ears.
  Your breath and dick brush the door
  As you stand at the threshold and wonder,
  If you should knock and ask to borrow
  A cup of raw sugar? You don't need much,
  Just a cup to dip your fingers in sweet stickiness,
  Just enough to still your parched trembling lips.

The Man in the Moon 1

Who's up at 2 am?
    The midnight oil has long burned out.
    Sleep and sex roll restless
    On worn mattresses.
    Dreams escape open eyes
    Shadows rattle the door
    Three o'clock is the witching hour
    Red ashes float from patios
    Eyes across the courtyard catch you breathing.
    You look away only to look again.
    You know your lonely mattress would enjoy the company
    And your lilac-scented air could use some funk.
    But the night won't last a lifetime, so
    You slip back into your room and wonder,
    What if there is a man in the moon?

The Man in the Moon 2

Through the open window, the Crown Plaza beckons
　　In red neon stars just beyond rooftops and
　　Night colored trees.
　　My room is dark, but my window yawns
　　Letting in silver moonlight.
　　Masculine voices rise from the balcony below.
　　The conversation is peppered with
　　Black bitches and white "hoes."
　　Smoke drifts in through the open window.
　　I have been hypnotized all night
　　By visions of prancing horses.
　　My only relief is self-sacrifice.
　　I drop my pants and aim at the man in the moon.
　　Those horses rear up on hind legs,
　　Their tails swat lilies and flies
　　Their cocks drown the grass.
　　In a moment, I call his name—
　　The one in the moon,
　　Smiles and swallows every drop.

Night Clothes

The best time to be naked is 3:00 am
    Black velvet skin is the proper attire
    As you stand on your balcony
    Stroking the night
    A little drink, a little smoke, a little lonely.
    There ought to be other men
    Standing on their porches too
    Aiming the red tips of their cigarettes
    At you.

A Good Dog

The neighbor beats his dog at 3AM
   and he don't stop
   I hear her tail beating the wall
   and he don't stop
   She gnaws on his bone
   and he don't stop
   All night long she whines
   and he don't stop
   Her collar and chain drags the floor
   and he don't stop
   She begs at the table
   and he don't stop
   She rolls over and plays dead
   and he don't stop
   She fetches his slippers
   and he don't stop
   She trees his birds
   and he don't stop
   She has his puppies
   and he don't stop
   All I hear in the wee hours is
   Bitch, bitch, bitch!
   And he don't stop.

Poem On A Horse

At 3 AM I wrote a poem on a horse.
    He told me to.
    He said, I want my ass to be artfully used.
    What they write on tombstones is bullshit
    But what you write on the left flank
    I'll let Jesus read.
    So I wrote:
    Brown hills grow berries ripening
    In summer sun. The sweet juice runs down my chin
    Turns to wine, sweeter than anything
    That started with water.
    "The Lord will be offended,"
    The horse neighed.
    "Who said he would read this poem?"
    I asked.

Eating....

corn on the cob at 3 AM
    that witching bitching hour
    when everything conceived is immaculate
    until the shit hits the fan
    nine months later.
    "Oh no baby you can't go back.
    I've let you live
    My coat hanger, unbent,
    is wrapped in fox
    in the closet."
    So here you are five decades later
    teeth gnawing on a corn on the cob
    You'd rather it had been
    that tall thing whose hips wrote poems.
    But hey these days eating is about surviving
    loving ain't about Jack'd
    Oh no not that
    I mean loving ain't ... isn't ... is
    slipping between your fingers.
    And now you're finished with the corn
    but the cob ... is it a possibility?

Club Boyland

So much lonesomeness after the club
    Shuts off the jazzing lights—
    makes one wonder if there was a point to all
    the flash and glitter and the new shoes
    giving your feet the blues.
    After the hug dap hug dap hug dap
    And the bourbon has diluted the blood,
    Three AM is the lonely hour
    except for crickets and the cars
    whizzing down the freeway
    and your heart beating solo under the sheets.
    You tell your hand to be still,
    the night's seen enough futility
    Perhaps tomorrow. Perhaps tomorrow.

Mattress on a Street Corner

It's 3 AM
    For those who can't make it
    From the bar
    To the car,
    There's love to be made
    Under the lamplight
    Under the moon's sight.
    Stars witness, and twinkle
    Their blue bright approval.
    Don't worry about the stop sign.
    Red is the color of love
    As you get down on this bed
    Of satin and rusty springs.

Nightmare Dreams

At 3 AM I hide poems under the mattress from him—
    The monster who shakes my shoulders and
    Fucks me in the ass.
    "3am is a bad hour for love," I say.
    The monster doesn't agree.
    The door clicks. "Show me a poem," he says.
    "The lord is my shepherd,
    I shall not want," I chant
    He backs off.
    "Tomorrow is another night," he says
    Before the door rattles in his wind.

3AM Dilemma

Did he say take three pills or thirty?
    "There's a lifetime of difference," a voice says.
    "Doctors don't know everything,"
    I say back.

A Dog and a Nightmare

Who is this that comes in the dark,
    Who presses against the small of my back,
    And shoulders? I want to kiss him,
    But instead I curse and shout the twenty-third psalm,
    "The Lord is my shepherd,
    I shall not want!"
    Sometimes he leaves right away
    And sometimes he lingers longer
    Turned on by my struggle.
    He digs his fingers into my ass.
    I look forward to his coming
    Not the Lord's but this thing
    I look forward to him mashing me into the mattress.
    When he's had enough,
    I hear bedroom door go thump
    And my ass twitches a little.
    "A man is a dog and a nightmare," my mother said once.
    I agree, "a dog and a nightmare."

Duckbill Platypus 3 AM

And I'm lying awake thinking about the duckbill platypus
    Is it a duck or beaver? Is it a quack?
    Does he love his parents June Cleaver and Donald Duck?
    You know she thought about scrambling his ass in a teaspoon
    Of hot sauce to hide her infidelity. But the Duck said let it be let it
be
    How does he eat? Who does he eat?
    What's his politics? Does he talk out of both sides of his mouth?
    If it were a man what sport would he play?
    I see a career in swimming or Frisbee. What's his kink in bed?
    Hmmm with a mouth like that I bet he's into spanking.
    It's 3 AM. Why is my dick all up in the duckbill platypus' head
instead of yours?
    Why baby? Why?

Uber Women

I drive around at night,
    Pick up lonely women,
    Take them home, and
    Watch them open their doors.
    I stand at their windows,
    As they throw bras and panties
    At my black moon face.
    Some tuck in and cuddle bears
    Others leap into the quilts and weep.
    One does herself better than a man
    Could ever do
    With no regrets and morning breath residue.
    These are the women I drive all night long.

Mystery 3AM

I wonder where I am?

Thirst

It's way past 3 AM
    and I would not should not could not
    do what I ought not. So I did not
    Then, I thought, do it anyway.
    So I can, shall, and will
    walk unlike an Egyptian
    and get my lazy hee haw
    a glass of water.
    (note to self: Stop writing)

LOVE SONGS

LOVE DOCTOR

That Doctor ain't got no license
    He practice love on the bootleg side
    Aint got no license
    Steals hearts just to get to the ass
    When he done got through
    You say, Lord my name Skinny Roo
    Love you so hard you change your name
    You can't sit down for days
    You dance all around the moon
    Singing Al Green tunes
    Love and happiness
    Three days later you touch your cold phone
    Look up in the mirror and your heart be gone
    You call them digits that doctor wrote down
    Ain't no such number in town.
    That doctor aint got no license
    Lord that doctor aint got license
    There you go trippin out to the graveyard
    Looking for some kind of heart to fill up
    The hole in your breast
    Lord, Lord. That doctor aint had no license at all
    You got your 45 just in case
    You run into that no license son of a bitch
    Love and happiness make you do wrong
    All night long.

I Know Why The Caged Bird Went Crazy

The thing you love is a prison,
    Hands hold you like iron bars.
    You bathe under watchful pastel blue eyes
    But hate those eyes and
    Want freedom over yonder.
    You love to love, because
    You fear freedom.
    You hate the freedom you love,
    Because you know
    Wings can fail under the sun's gaze.
    We want to be in one another's dungeons
    Yet are grateful when we're not.
    We curse the night and shadows
    Dancing outside our open windows
    As we lockdown our hearts.

Living Through Your Hair

I want to live vicariously
   Through your locs
   Want to feel, see, touch, smell, and taste
   All that you do in bed, on a beach,
   in the alley, in dark anonymous rooms.
   I will be there when your eyes first meet his
   When he's late for that first date
   And your flowers go flaccid in the vase.
   I will run through your rooms
   When he chases you naked.
   I will watch him cook your breakfast
   Wearing nothing but an apron.
   I will scream when he grabs a fist full of me
   As he plunges deep inside you.
   I'll sneak out on the balcony with you
   To smoke and fuck at 3 a.m.
   I'll let him comfort you when life
   Throws bitter tears in your face.
   When you moan I will hear and moan with you.
   When you come, I will sing your song.
   When he kisses you, I will kiss him back.
   If he strikes you I will fall to the floor
   While you whip his ass.
   If he leaves you, I will mourn with you
   And carry his scent when you travel
   To the stars.

The Seven Spells

Spell #1
All them spells you cast—
the rat's heart fed to the cat,
the jism stained drawers you burned,
the fingernail clippings you boiled and ate,
the hair you rolled and smoked—
all them spells decades ago
didn't bring you no man
and certainly not *that* man
you worshipped with candles and incantations
But suddenly here he is and you
with naked arms cradling naked waist
and you didn't do a damned thing.

Spell #2
Your heart is the moon full
yesterday it was a slice of light
tomorrow it is the sickle's sharp edge.
Spell #3
If psychosis drive you to rant
and deludes you to thinking
you are the king of all that glitters
on Saturday night, Then are the spells
I asked Sister Aretha to cast
and make you say you love me
all in vain?

Spell #4

    At the clinic on the exam table
    you lie with feet in stirrups
    sucking a lollipop and jacking
    while the doctor extracts
    dried old men from your rectum.
    They call your ass the graveyard
    Many entered. You shat out their hearts
    and kept the ivory bones.

Spell #5
God has left me to be at the mercy
of St. Michael cloaked in daggers and tongues
and beauty that out shines the stars
Lord, what now

Spell #6

Odd numbers work well
    for one person, but not two.
    We revere seven and deny thirteen
    So here is written six spells and not seven
    I asked the madam to cast two lots
    One to make you love me
    and one to make me love me too.

Lips

I want your lips on my lips
    on my naked neck and at the end of my nipple
    hanging on, baby, for dear life. I have no milk—
    I'm a man, but I have life in my nipple.
    I offer my fingers for you to suck
    with your thick pussy lips.
    When my fingers are well wet with your saliva,
    they go one digit at a time up your mannish honeypot,
    where my lips hummed symphonies and my tongue
    ballet danced last night.
    Do you remember what you said to me
    when I came up for air?
    "Man, you smell like my Mama's chit'lins."
    It didn't hurt me when you didn't offer reciprocity.
    Your lips on my lips on my naked neck
    hanging on, baby, for dear life was enough.

Tell Me a Bedtime Story
Once upon a time
Eye to eye
Two lovers lazed about
Gazing into their soft Saturday eyes.
A hand reached toward the sun
Streaming like sliced peaches
Through the venetian blinds
Fingers rested in chest hair, so soft
Lips locked, tongues battled, surrendered, retreated to run
Down necks toward chest and candied nipple
The room muted the ocean's roar.
Walls echoed soft sighs
Belly buttons let go giggles.
From ticklish spots sprang laughter and resignation.
By now cocks were hard and pressed belly to belly
Knees like russet potatoes
Aimed toward the skylight
A tongue told the cock to wait,
And found its sweet spot, the ass
That smelled like Mama's chitlins boiling on the stove.
Tongue plunged deep, rested, backed out,
Thought for a moment, and drove back in
Until the cock whispered,
"Okay, that's enough, Daddy. My turn."
The cock entered with ease
Met no resistance
Was guided by the footprints of soldiers
Who had gone on before.
It curved to the right
To take the road less traveled,
Labored until the nuts banged dizzy

Against the wall.
Heels met over the broad back
The eyes shut themselves
But the lips and tongues
Desired to dance again.
The room growled, cursed, and drowned the ocean.
After the last sigh and looking at their sticky fingers
One of them told a story of Mama's cake batter.
"It was so much sweeter than this bitterness
we lick from our fingers this morning,
so much sweeter and yellow like the sun
so much sweeter and creamier.
I'd go all day without washing my hands
And suck my fingers until they wrinkled.
Baby, will you bake me a cake tonight?"

Sweetness
When you dip almonds in honey
And invite robins to serenade
And the flowers to dance around his hair
Soft as lamb's wool
And curled as cupid's
You are in the world of youth dew.
I await for him to offer me
A bit of sweetness, a bit of glee.

Writing Poems
I don't know
If I want to die
Writing poems
Or sucking cock
He said,
"Write me a poem
as long as my dick, daddy."
I wrote
"I love you."
One hundred times
One hundred times
One hundred times
Until the pen ran out of paper.

Incomplete Stories

The Preacher and Some Bucks

It's tough these days for a boy in college. Ever since Dean Porter straightened me out, my grades have been in the top ten percent of the entire State University. I will graduate cum laud or maybe summa cum laude. I like them words "cum laude." That's what us boys say in our jack circle to the slow poke in the group, "Cum lawd cum!" Anyway the budget cuts from Uncle Sam done shorted my grant money. Moms be trying to send me some change. Her little buck fifty a month helps. But then again sometimes it feels like pissing in the sea. A nigga have expenses. Gotta keep my gear up to date, especially my footgear. The Dean arranged for me to get a job in the library. That worked out aight 'til the head librarian came at me with an indecent proposal. All I gotta say is, this nigga ain't for dressing like no slave in ripped up ass-out jeans to cut no yard, even if you promise me some mind blowing head. I ain't catering to some white dude's fantasy.

But like I was saying, my money's been real short lately. In fact all my boy's money been short except for that nigga Leroy. Now that nigga don't call himself Leroy. He go by the name "Cable TV." He calls himself that because he got more hustles than Xfinity has channels. Cable started at State University poor as shit. He dressed so bad, sometimes homeless people offered him a dollar. But then all of a sudden that nigga started coming up. Nigga went from Wrangler jeans to True Religions overnight. Got out of them boat sneakers and into Jordan's. He wears real diamond studs in his ears.

One day after I kicked his ass at the gym playing hoops and as we dried off after our shower, I noticed Cable pulling some Gucci draws over his ass. I say, "Nigga where you get the money to get some Gucci draws?" Cable looked at me and smiled.

"Channel six on your cable box, nigga. Channel six answered my prayers. And it will answer yours." He bent over and slapped his ass in my face.

I told him, "Watch out nigga I'll tear a hole right through them Gucci's and split your ass with this ten and a half."

"You don't say? You better pick your teeth with it first, before you think about putting that wee thing in anybody's ass."

He finished dressing and scooted out the door. Me and my boys going to get drunk and take Cable down a notch or two after we find out how he make his money. Nigga always throwing his ass in our faces. If we didn't like girls, we would have already took care of him.

Back in my dorm room I cuts on the TV and pop in my favorite Porn DVD of white girls getting fucked by big ass black dudes. After my jack and while staring at my nut on the ceiling, I'm feeling kind of like shit because I'm broke. I wonder what's on channel six that's making Cable so rich these days. I pick up the remote and start flipping channels. I land on channel six. I say to myself, what the fuck? I don't see nothing but ads. This shit is the Craigslist channel. I didn't know they even had they own channel. But I guess anything is possible if they have a jewelry channel and all them infomercials. They even got a whole TV show selling a dumb ass vacuum cleaner. Well anyway I look through the Craigslist ads with my remote, and wonder what the hell Cable see on here that makes money. I aint got no raggedy ass car to sell, nor do I want to fix nobody's computer. I'm about to turn Channel Six off when I see something called Personals. I check the shit out. This about some sex shit. I click on it and they gots all kind of choices—M4W W4M MW4MW MW4W MM4W MM4MM M4TS MM4anything. There's more alphabets than in a bowl of Campbell's alphabet soup.

I click on some of the ads and start reading them. Some people be doing some perverted shit. White dudes talking about playing with dogs and drinking piss. That shit ain't for me. Now I'll eat the hell out of some pussy. I did let somebody suck my dick once when I was seventeen, but that's as far as on the downlow I want to go.

Then I spots one ad that says, College BOY LIKES OLDER. I click on it. I say damn I recognize that ass with that red birthmark on it. I just saw that ass. It's Cable's ass. His ad says he likes the company of older generous$ men. I say fuck that's how that nigga been upgrading. Shit man I can't do no shit like that. Even though me and my boys mess around, I still got a rep with the ladies. Speaking of ladies, that's another reason why I be broke—Brianna over there at Spelman College. Big Concert Battle coming up with Trey Songz and Chris Brown and she want to go. Damn nosebleed tickets is a buck fifty. A nigga needs to have money these days. Anyway I read on further and something catches my eye:

GENROU$ DI$CRETE MAN WANT$ TO MEET $ERIOU$ COLLEGE DUDE$. COUNT THE DOLLAR IGN THAT'S HOW $ERIOUS I AM. CALL AND FIND OUT WHAT EACH DOLLAR $IGN STAND$ FOR. MIGHT BE 10 OR A 100 IF YOU'RE THE RIGHT DUDE AND HIGHLY DISCREET. CALL 404-559-$$$$

I counted them fifteen dollar signs and did the math. Damn! A chance to make fifteen hundred Benjamins! Whoever this person is, they must have some serious Bill Gates kind of money to offer a nigga fifteen hundred dollars to get out of his draws. Yeah them fifteen dollar signs was looking real good to a nigga. I called the number. A voice answered "Rebirth Ministries." My tongue got caught in the roof of my mouth and refused to budge. I thought this some bullshit prank ad. I was about to hang up, when the voice said, "Rebirth Ministries. How can I help you young man?" Shit. How he know I was a dude without me even speaking? So I spoke up. "I was watching channel six and ..."

"You're straight and all boy?"

"Yeah..."

"That's cool."

He then asked me to describe myself and my dick. He said my chiseled abs and tight stomach was righteous. He said we might have a deal like I was selling a car or some shit. But he had a special request. He asked if I had a girl. Hell yeah, I said. Then he said something that made me want to drop the phone in the toilet and drown his ass—even though you can't do no shit like that.

"Man, I ain't asking my girl to join us. Nigga, is you crazy?"

"No. No. Not in the flesh. Only in the spirit. I'll explain what I mean, when I meet you."

"I don't know if I want to meet your ass."

"How many dollar signs did you count, young man?"

"Fifteen. But that don't mean shit. I ain't getting my girl involved in this."

"Listen, just for us to meet, I'll give you ten dollars for each dollar sign and to prove I'm not a pervert."

I agreed to meet him. After all, a buck fifty would help out on them concert tickets. Me and Brianna could eat popcorn if we got hungry. And dessert wasn't no problem with a freak like her.

****

I slid into the leather seats in the Preacher's Bentley. He was parked a block from Brianna's dorm room. I was exhausted as hell. I felt like I had been playing full court basketball.

"Did you work that pussy?"

"Yeah," I answered kind of sullen-like.

"Let me see that dick."

I pulled it out and it still glistened with Brianna's pussy juices.

"That's what I'm talking about. I can't wait to get you to the office." He told me about how he didn't get no action from his wife. She's the first lady and got her own ministry and shit. Besides she did her women's thing and he did his "man thang." Imagine this from a dude who got on national TV and said God uses fags to clean the toilets in hell.

We rolled to the church. The preacher pushed the gate opener and the gates slid open wide like Brianna's legs. We got out and he unlocked a side door and lead me into his office. The office is sickening. His desk was gold and mahogany and as big as my whole dorm room. A gold chandelier hung over it. A huge leather sofa surrounded a mirrored coffee table. There was oil paintings of scenes from the bible all over the room. Near naked Jesus on the cross; Jonathan and David hugging; David dressed like Tarzan slinging a rock into Goliath's eye; Roman soldiers driving chariots and fighting—all males. The paint was so oily they looked like they was sweating. He went to his bar and offered me a glass of "holy water" I said no. He sat down at his desk and beckoned for me. I went over and stood in front of him. He sniffed my crotch through my jeans. Then he asked me to take everything off.

I did. He grabbed my dick and sniffed long and deep like he was trying to inhale all of Brianna's pussy smell. Then he told me to hop on his desk and lay back. He put my feet on the arms of his big chair so that my legs were wide open. Me and my girl's smells filled up the room. I felt guilty. It's like a part of her is in this room naked with me. My dick could barely rise. The preacher saw my trouble and made a suggestion. I almost jumped off the desk and went upside his head. He wanted me call Brianna while he sucked my dick. "Hell no," I said.

But then he told me to tell her I missed her and I was jacking my dick thinking about her and I needed the sound of her voice to help me get to that point of no return.

I told him "Fuck no" and started to rise. He laid three Benjamins by the phone. Now I'm a practical mother fucker. Brianna really ain't had to be in the room. And fuck, she's kind of freaky her damn self. I ain't forgot that time she and her best girl was kind of drunk and she got to bragging about how big my dick was. Well they both went down on me. She swears it never happened. I picked up the phone.

"Baby, I love you like a fat kid love cake," I said to her. I always say some corny Fifty-Cent shit to her to try and make her laugh.

"Boy what you talkin' about?"

"I miss you, baby."

"Nigga, you just left here. I told you, you could've stayed over. Just have your ass out before six when the RA gets up. But no, you just had to leave."

"I know you did, baby. And I'm sorry. I thought I was going to study, but I got to thinking about what we did and how good it was."

"I done sucked your dick before."

"It was something special this time. It was like you was married to my dick."

"Nigga you crazy," she laughed.

Talking to Brianna made my dick rise. Me and the preacher got a whiff of her pussy still on my dick. Our nostrils flared. I kept talking to Brianna and she got into the groove. The preacher started licking my inner thighs and I was soon brick. His tongue flickered over my balls and lingered in that space between my balls and asshole. I moaned like a sinner in church. Then he let that tongue flicker over my knob head and my pee hole. My body trembled and that vein that squirts that love juice got rigid. He eased up. Then he went after the shaft of my dick like a dog gnaws on a bone. All you could hear was "Shlock, shlock."

"What's that noise?" Brianna asked.

"I'm jacking, baby, to your love sounds."

Then she really got into it. She put the phone down there so I could hear them fingers working that pussy. At the same time the preacher man was working over my dick. He pressed the speaker button so he could hear Brianna. Her voice her moans and thighs clapping together made him take my ten all the way to his throat. That nigga was sounding like a bull snorting. He backed off a little every time I was near to coming.

Finally with all that action of Brianna moaning over the phone and this nigga sucking my dick, I exploded. I felt my nut hit the back of his throat. He didn't even cough or miss a beat. Just swallowed like he was drinking a glass of milk. He eased up off my dick after he had guzzled the last drop and we listened as Brianna came. Shit my dick was still hard. And when I heard Brianna call my name and heard her bed squeaking like a car with some bad springs, one more drop of cum shot out and hit the preacher dead in his eye. He bounced to the bathroom to wash his eye out. I laid there on his desk with my head in his pile of money and stared at that golden chandelier. In the glass beads I saw rainbow colors. After the concert, I plan to make Brianna pay dearly for my sins.

Banana Pudding

I peered trough the window after the doorbell gonged and wondered why my gentleman caller was wearing a yellow raincoat. The sky was brilliantly blue and the sun shined so hard the flowers in my neighbors yard looked plastic pinwheels. Reluctantly, I opened the door.

"I hadn't heard the weatherman say anything about rain today. I said looking him up and down."

He stood tall, but bent a little at the waist. He looked at me through dark eyes that appeared like bruises in the middle of his smooth face. He hesitated as if contemplating running away. A blue bandana with the words "Chiquita Rocks" fit tight on his head. I smiled a smile that matched the sun and the yellow suit. My visitor relaxed, stamped his black boot on the welcome mat, and hopped across the threshold on one foot.

"This ain't no raincoat. It's a yellow summer coat. I like yellow."

"I see you do. It's a great color for a warm day."

"It's a great color period. You should see my friends hanging out at the grocers all green acting like young boys. They didn't believe the tree. The tree said we wouldn't be green long. The tree didn't lie. I'm a man already."

"The tree?"

"Yeah, the tree."

I tried my best to decipher this bit of conversation that flowed from the bruise of a mouth. Maybe he's smoked something, I said to myself. I offered him a refreshment.

"Would you like something to drink?"

"Anything but a banana daiquiri."

"Brandy?"

"Hell no. My cousin died in a concoction made with brandy."

"No I meant would you like to listen to Brandy? I have her latest CD," I lied

The bruised eyes stared at me. " Brandy aint did a CD in years. I don't take too kindly to those jokes. I saw my cousin drenched in brandy and set afire. It was not a pretty sight. Water will do for me."

"Would you like a slice of...hmm maybe not."

"Would I like a slice of what?"

"I was going to say banana bread, but I thought I'd better not."

"You thought right. I'm beginning to wonder about me coming here."

"Why? Are you afraid I'm a cereal killer?" I broke out in a macabre Vincent Price laugh." My guest stood straight up from the couch.

"I think I'd better go."

"Oh please don't go. I'm so sorry."

He made a hop toward the door.

"Please, please, I'm so sorry. I haven't had a man in so long. I'm just being giddy and silly. Please stay. In your online profile you said you were so horny."

I tugged at his arm and led him to my laptop sitting on the dining room table. I shook the mouse and the screen came alive with ADAM4EVERYTHING. "Look here is your profile." I read it to him,

> *"12.5 and ready for everything*
> *If your ass can take it*
> *Your mouth will sing*
> *Nut guaranteed*
> *No faking it."*

He relaxed and sat down on the couch. "Well you do have a nice ass. Bet it's never had a banana big as me."

"No it hasn't. It's never had anything as big as you," I lied in my most sincere voice. A cucumber smelling like shit and slathered in Vaseline snoozed in the vegetable bin of my refrigerator. He was a Thirteen. The guy at the farmer's market said he was the runt of a prize-winning genus. "If this is the runt, I'd hate the see the biggest." I said to the farmer's market guy.

"An elephant couldn't take it," He winked and wrapped the runt in a paper bag.

Back to my banana. "It would be kind of nice if we introduced ourselves. I'm Henry." I held out my hand.

"I'm Waldo."

"Walnut?"

"No no not walnut, Waldo, man. I hope you're not being funny."

"No not at all. I have a slight hearing problem."

"Well we've heard each other talk enough. We need to get down to business."

"It's nothing wrong wit being pleasant to one another. I love small talk. Gets me in the mood for loving."

"Uh yeah, I guess. Can you turn up the AC? It's getting kind of warm in here."

"I looked at him for a moment. His skin so beautiful and yellow was getting a few tiny brown spots. He batted away a gnat. I smiled. "Banana pudding for dessert," I said to myself.

I touched his smooth skin. "So what ideas do you have for my ass, big boy?"

"Slide in and out."

"Yes and?"

"Slide in and out."

"Yes! I love that and?"

"Slide in and out."

"Okay," I said to myself, "Maybe I should have stuck with the cucumber. At least he had that rugged skin that tickled my asshole."

Waldo sensed my disappointment. "Look at me man, I'm just a banana. My arms are pretty much non-existent. I ain't got much of a mouth and tongue. But what I do, I do good and that's slide in and out of ass holes like yours. If you want more take your ass back to ADAM4EVERYTING and get yourself a Zucchini squash or a cucumber. Plenty of them on there hanging around waiting for creeps with imaginations. I'm a down-to-earth man."

"I want you. I chose you," I said in my most sultry reassuring voice."

Dinner at Fred's was at eight. It was already five thirty. If I was going to make banana pudding and give it time to gel in the fridge I needed to hurry. I touched Waldo. He was smooth and hard all over, except for a little soft spot near his belly.

"Um the AC, don't forget the AC."

"Yes of course." I got up and turned the dial from seventy-two to seventy nine. I came back into the room shivering to give the impression that cold air was blowing through the vents. Waldo seemed reassured, though I noticed a few more brown spots on his "summer coat."

"Come with me." I grabbed one of Waldo's tiny hands

As I led him toward the bedroom, we passed my kitchen. He glanced at the top of the refrigerator at the three big boxes of vanilla wafers and hesitated. I looked up at the fridge too. "I'm glad Kroger had those on sale," I said. "My nieces and nephews love those things." He relaxed.

In the bedroom, I quickly stripped out of my tank top and shorts. I stood there all bronze and naked for Waldo to see and patted my vanilla-wafer-brown ass cheeks. "Come on big boy, get out of that yellow coat.

"I fuck better with my clothes on. It's kind of my thing. But it do feel a tad warmer in here."

"Whatever floats your ice cream boat. It'll be as cold as a banana split in a minute in here."

"What I tell you about making jokes about me?" Waldo threw me across the bed and yanked his bandana off. He managed to use his short arms to pin my ankles to my rail headboard. I looked in the mirror and thought of a turkey about to be stuffed. I loved it. Waldo drilled all of his twelve and a half into me. He alternated between long and deep strokes to jack hammer pounding.

"Yes! Yes, Daddy!" I cried out over and over.

"Anymore banana jokes, boy?"

"No daddy no. Ooh Daddy pound that ass good."

"I heard you been fucking a cucumber behind my back."

"No Daddy, it's just been you."

"You're a liar." And Waldo drilled deep sliding next to my prostate. Electrical currents shot through my body. My toes tingled. I screamed and begged for mercy all the while wanting more as Waldo shoved his twelve and a half into me. After fifteen minutes of this pounding, I couldn't hold back. I shot a load all over my chest and face. Waldo shuddered, shook, and pulled out. The heat of my ass had turned him brown all over. He gasped for air.

"It's damn hot in here, man. Did you turn up the AC like I asked?

"Yes I did Daddy O. I put it on Seventy-nine."

"I wanted it colder hot hotter, fool. I'm ripening. Turn that AC down to sixty quick!"

"Aw Daddy. You just need to take off these soggy wet clothes." I nuzzled his chest with my cum filled face. He tried to push me away, but he soft and helpless. I started peeling his clothes off.

"Leave me alone, you evil pervert."

"Aw Daddy, it's going to be all right. Just let your Henry take these ugly wet clothes off you." I peeled him out of his clothes. Underneath he was still white. Although I saw a soft bruise near his nipple."

"Oh Lord, what have I gotten myself into?" Waldo began to whimper.

"It's all right Daddy, Just lie with me in this nice warm air." I got up and opened the blinds wider so that the evening sun blazed in.

"Lord why? Why me, Jesus? Why didn't you make me a normal banana so the bees could spread my seeds to that cute banana tree two rows over? We could have raised some fine plantains. But instead here I am ripening in some punks bed." Waldo bawled.

"Well it could be worse. You could have wound up in the zoo and been fed to the apes. I've seen what they do to bananas and it ain't a pretty sight," I reminded him.

Waldo bawled some more. I looked at my pig-faced alarm clock. It was six thirty. I dragged a rapidly ripening Waldo to the floor and sat my naked ass on his face. It mashed easily. I continued down his body until he was just a smushed smashed thing. I then went into the kitchen and got a big spoon and bowl and scraped Waldo off the floor. A bit of him lingered between my ass cheeks. I scraped that off too. I got down two boxes of Vanilla wafers off the fridge and went to work on that pudding.

Dinner later that night at Fred's was crab cakes and boring conversation. I unwrapped my dessert pan. Fred wrinkled his nose.

"Eeew, Henry, Your banana pudding looks good but it smells like shit."

"Whatever, girl. Waldo loves it.

"Next time, bring Waldo for dessert."

I laughed and scooped a big dollop of pudding onto my plate.

My Private Toilet

I'm very rich. I'm into oil and gas. Love that black oozy stuff. I'm very clean. The most famous restaurants have served me the most famous dishes. Foi a grosse, caviar, port au vin 1933 $3000 a bottle. I serve it to Slaughter. I love the taste of of port au vin gushing out of him. I buy very expensive colognes. Such a habit is a necessity.

I am single. That's a necessity also. I travel all over the world looking at my oil fields, making deals, and buying shit to fill up this 15000 square foot shit hole I live in. Fifteen thousand square feet and the only room I love holds a toilet. And not the four hundred square foot shimmering glittering thing with the waterfall shower and aquarium. I had the lawn man build one next to his tool shed full of oiled parts fertilizer, ropes, and chains. It is the way a toilet should be—rough concrete floors, unlidded commode, low to the ground. I had installed a claw footed tub and a single basin on which a single bar of Lifebuoy soap rests. That soap and that tub are the things of my childhood. The grandparents lived by that soap. *"It'll make a pig smell like a rose garden,"* gramps liked to say as he scrubbed my behind. *"Beauford, this is good for getting all the tar outta your bowels,"* was Gram's favorite saying. The warm enema bag feeling like a cat on my belly. My legs rested in the grooves in the back of the dining room chair pulled up to my bed my ass cradled in a white and steel bed pan. She'd unlatch the nozzle and let just a little water in at a time until my belly felt like I'd eaten a bowl of her gumbo.

I named my oil company Tar Oil. I owe that to Gramps and Gram too. Something spooked the cows one day and one fell into a pit of foul sulphur smelling muck. Oil. A month later Gram had a 1970 fleet wood brougham to drive herself to the beauty parlor. They built a new house. Gramps turned the old one into a two-story tool shed. A 900 square foot two story looks mighty small standing next to a French chateau.

May was the man hired to take care of running the land and herding the hundred or so cows, three dozen horses, and a buffalo roaming about. May was short for Mason. Mason was for the thirty-three degrees Mason his mother named him after. He had a peculiar color for a colored man. Well that's what gramps called him. All I can say is gramps progressed the best he could after getting used to black people having civil rights. Mason was the color shit when you have a fever—yellowish tan. In a certain light he could make you sick to look at him. The moonlight turned him gold like a coin. May and his wife Rachel came to the ranch—we called it that—out of the blue—a blue sky day and riding in a 1960 blue ford fair lane. They had sawed off part of the top over the back seat and nailed a big sheet of plywood across the open part making them a mini pickup truck before

Japan sent then Datsuns to America. Flush with oil money Gramps and Gram allowed themselves the luxury of a full time hired man and a woman in the kitchen. Everything else was day help—one or two days here and there.

May and Rachel had a peculiar relationship. She stayed in the chateau with us sleeping in the no purpose room behind the kitchen. May made a place in the two-story tool shed. A big room with the toilet and bath tub peeking through the studs where a wall of Sheetrock used to be. Gramps said he never understood why husband and wife couldn't sleep in the same bed, much less under the same roof.

"Maybe it's his color," Gram remarked. He sickens me to look at sometimes."

"Well I'm sure he was that color when she married him."

"No woman would ever marry a man that color. He must have caught the jaundice."

"Rachel calls him stinky," I piped up.

"How would she know how he smelled? I ain't seen 'em standing next to each other in the six months they been here," Gramps said.

"How do you know what she calls him, Lemon Pie?" Gram asked me as she picked at her eggs that weren't burned.

"I heard her."

"Well don't go listening to too much of that nigger talk. It'll ruin you," Gramps huffed.

"Benjamin Scott Lee!" Granny screeched. "The boy don't need to hear that."

"I hoped you done wiped your shitty ass before coming in this house," Rachel hissed at her husband one day when he stood at the back screen door with his toolbox in hand. One of the five commodes in the chateau was stopped up. "But then a toilet is right up your alley," she said twisting her nose at his back walking by her.

Later that night as I sat on that same toilet watching the violent blue water wash away the soapy water mixed with my brown pellets of shit, I wondered why a toilet would fascinate anyone. Although this was a nicer toilet compared to the ones at St. John's boys prep—ours had a gold handle to match the gold Grecian etching around the bowl versus the pot shaped things with black seats that the boys kept the janitors unstopping—still a toilet was a toilet, even if the seat was heated. A voice in me said not to bother asking Gramps or Gram that question. Children know what secrets to keep from parents. A whole other world takes place at school, but when parents ask, "How was your day?" They get a humped shoulder, or the perfunctory, "We learned some math and something about photosynthesis. I'm hungry." There's nothing about Aaron's head being dunked in the pissy toilet because his family invited a black preacher to dinner and he was half Jewish.

There are other secrets I kept. Gramps bought me a pair of WWII binoculars from an army surplus store in Dallas. "We could see them kikes eating sauerkraut 20 miles away with these things, boy." One lens was as clear as a cloudy day. But the other one, if I rolled the focus wheel far to the right and used one eye did let me see the freight trains crossing the river about two miles away—if the sky was blue enough. In the summer time I could lie on my bed and watch May over in the horse pasture. Gramps didn't care if I had the window raised high like it was ok to cool the yard from them three-ton AC units cooling the chateau. He didn't care too much what May did to the horses as long as he kept them shined as Gram's caddy. He and Gram spent their days in one of the three parlors watching *Let's Make A Deal*. I didn't care much about the horses and focused the binoculars on the new house being built 300 acres over on the land Gramps sold to a housing developer. The developer ten years ago, had turned his nose up at that smelly tarry swamp Gramps had offered to sell him. Thank God.

So it was me lying on my bed watching tractor trailers hauling in what look like match sticks that was turning into "matchbox houses" granny remarked. My binoculars caught May's back looking as yellow as autumn corn. Then I saw it wasn't just his back the sun was lighting up. He stood on top of a hay bale with his pants just below his knees. His hand rested on his side with his elbow jutting out. His right hand was hidden from view in front of his pants. I thought at first he was taking a piss. But then I noticed his hand jerking like Gramps palsied hand, but only faster. He then leaned back for about a minute. I shifted my binoculars and noticed the black horse tail lifted cock swinging like a toy bat and piss gushing like water out of the garden hose from between his legs. I shifted back to May. My binoculars filled with his tanned buttocks as he reached for his jeans. That's another thing I never mentioned to Gram and Gramps. Children know how to keep secrets.

Gram died then Rachel...(To be continued)

The Editr

The cannonball patted her plump rare then stood in front of her and looked Amy in the eye.

"You make a nice Christmas dinner," he said smacking his lips loudly.

Amy instantly regretted using that cute but airhead travel agent she used to make her travel plans.

The cannonball opened his cupboard and accessed his seasons. He had lots of salt and pepper but no time and acumen. Some organo would be nice two, he thought.

"Well what kind of editor does my story need? Copy editor, development editor, or conceptual editor?" Jackson asked.

"It needs all of those things," Gretchen from the Kuhl Lipscomb Agency advised him.

"And perhaps a psychological editor as well."

"So you think my story is good?" Jackson asked all puppy-eyed.

Gretchen from Kuhl, Lipscomb stared out her window and made vacation plans. "London sounds nice," she thought. She had lost her appetite for New Guinea.

I CAN'T LIVE WITH OR WITHOUT YOU

U2

The Beast He Doesn't Tell His Friends About
    I want to be a young man's secret
    The beast he doesn't tell his friends about
    The thing he comes to see after midnight
    The dog who does things his mama
    Would scorn him for
    Though she taught him bawdy songs
    Hold tight, hold tight, mama I want some seafood tonight
    One leg in the east, one leg in the west,
    My man in the middle doing his best.
    I want to be the one whose tongue travels deep, deep
    Into his ass, past his loins
    And into his heart and linger there a moment.
    He might lie awake with his girl or boy
    Nesting in his arms, and suddenly think about
    My toothless mouth gripping his dick.
    He'll scratch his nuts and wake up his partner,
    But then give up because it won't be the same.
    His ass will sting where my hand smacked.
    He'll want his girl to rub it, scratch it,
    Spread warm oil deep inside,
    Massage his prostate
    But he's afraid she'll think he's weird
    And call him a punk.
    He'll yawn and think about how
    My dick felt in his mouth
    How he choked on the head
    He'll feel my hand gripping his neck
    And wiping my cum off his lips,
    He'll kiss his boyfriend and offer him some of me.
    When he eats his mama's lemon pound cake
    He'll remember the time he fed me cake laced with jism,

chocolate and cherries.
As he's shooting hoops with his boys
His ass will tremble at the touch of hands, guarding him
And he'll wonder if one is my hand.
When he shits, he'll remember taking me
All the way just yesterday
In my dark room with his ankles wrapped around my back.
He'll wonder if his bois have secrets like him,
Are old men placing them on altars
Of iniquity, swallowing their future generations,
Giving them secrets they'll take to their graves?
When he slips out the back door of my yellow shotgun house
He'll run fast to beat the morning sun just rising
Glimpsing his shadow and telling his secrets.

Daddy (Reprised)
He a bullnecked man, bald as a baby's ass
Thick glasses make him look like he full of daddy sweetness
But he a big bullnecked man,
Full of tricks with ropes and bottles
His favorite sport is the baby trick
You be the baby, ass all tied up knees touching your ears
You a cute lil dickens
He go *goo gah gah*
And you gurgle and wiggle your toes
Your ass hole
Cotton candy Pink,
Golden brown,
Black as a cave door—
Don't matter to him.
He a bullnecked man
Thick glasses make him look like daddy sweetness
This is his trick
He got one thick rope stretched across your mouth
All you can do is go *wah wah wah*
While daddy feed you that Pepsi bottle
Draped in a red white and blue sash
Wah wah wah you go
As he gently rocks your boat
You had asked for rough stuff
And no baby oil
But daddy knows best
Eyes all gentle with daddy sweetness,
When he get through
Y'all drank the Pepsi
The baby oil soothes your chapped lips.

Offerings

On Saturday I stand in the window cleaning the glass
In my draws and t-shirt torn.
I take in the whole Washington Avenue
And it takes in me. What can the law say?
I'm not naked. Females look the other way,
Except for teen girls who giggle.
Older men grimace and shake their heads.
It's the young hungry ones
Who look and see opportunity and possibility.
By evening time the curtains are closed
I'm in my back room entertaining Possibility and Opportunity.
I'm on these same knees that touch the prayer rail on Sunday
Right now it's evening Mass, and I'm receiving offerings.

Unscented Soap
Not a whiff of him
The Lavender Calamine, gone!
Just a wet towel
Lumped
Over the edge of the bath tub
Like a snoozing cat.
Now the other one hung around—
Cuddled.
I pawed his thin leg bone
Told him a story
About a preacher who killed a girl
Because he was in love
With her dude—
Stabbed her forty times
For each day and night
of the Lord's tears.
I listened to his story
Of when a taxicab struck him
And he flew through the air
Found holy ground a half block away
At the Power House Church of God
And knew that's where he was supposed to be.
He took a long time to shower—
Used some of that other ones
Unscented soap
I dried his shoulders and back
Watched him lotion himself—
Even down there glistened like
A stick of licorice.
Then,
Clothes on

Blue black scrubs like a morgue worker.
"Who's going to open that door?"
He hid his eyes from the glaring sun.
The question, "Will I see you again?" hung from my lips
Like crumbs
Him—
Not answering
Just a bar of soap left behind.

The Library After Midnight
Deserted Library toilet
full of niggas calling themselves MAN.
mAn aND nIGERS
scrawled in shit across the tiles.
"Where you going ol' gee
with them big toilet bowl lips?"
"I tipped in to piss," I plead.
"Save it pops
It's going back into your belly.
Take off everything and join the others."
They pinned me to the wall, spread eagled—
Professors and freshman caught in their trap.
Rough hands peeled my ass apart like red passion fruit.
They entered like Shaka Zulu's army.
"Zulu's army got drowned in the pissy sea,"
They chanted as I rode to Taurus
With an army of soldiers in my mouth.

Write A Poem While I Fuck You
Get some paper
Write a poem while I fuck you.
No,
Write a story while I fuck you.
Stories are longer. I love bedtime stories.
Yeah write about how it feels going in.
"Like the army passing between two hills..."
I like that. Oh!
But you didn't say how it felt in your mouth.
"Like trying to swallow a alligator."
I like that. My dick do look like an alligator.
Get some more paper.
Now, when I first kissed you...
What that felt like?
"Like butterflies lighting on my lips."
Cool... I see butterflies out our window
What's wrong?
You can't write while I fuck you?
I'll slow down. I want you to keep writing.
You need a hit of poppers?
Okay, now when I be licking your nipples—what that feel like?
"Like butterflies lighting on my chest."
Umm, say something else. You already said butterflies.
Maybe say something about lace and silk.
And when I be licking your ass...
What my tongue feel like?
"Like a rattle snake's tail."
I don't know. I don't like snakes.
I'm a let you slide on that one.
And when I kiss the back of your knees?
You said butterflies before.

Am I boring you?
Okay. Okay!
I know it's your story, but it's mine too, baby.
So what about when we do some real freaky stuff?
How do my piss taste?
"Like drinking a martini in a dark café."
No I don't know Nancy Wilson
"Guess who I saw today?"
I like the way you sang that, so soulful,
That made my dick hard.
I need some more of that Nancy Wilson.
And when I make you wear panties
And stand in the window
So niggas can see—what that feel like?
"Like a Jewish girl undressing in front of the Nazis."
What's all that about? Is that you or the poppers talking?
You got some scary shit in your head.
But I still want to fuck you in the window.
In broad daylight as ghetto streets stride by.
Yeah, in broad daylight as ghetto streets stride by.

To Dream The Impossible Dream
I want a horsey for Christmas
I'll keep him on the patio
Ride him in the living room
At 3AM while the neighbors sleep
We'll gallop all night break up
The tiles and wood floor
And then trot to the bedroom
And ride some more.
He can be black, brown, or white
I'll name him Goodnight or Goodknight
Yea he'll neigh and make a mess
But don't all horses do that?
I've read your stories about your stallion
Named Unfaithful.

The Cookie Monster

I need some young crazy nigga action
    Young wild haired black
    Crazy with lust and malice—
    A brain cell missing nigga
    The kind of wild eyed nigga
    Chasing your ass around the room
    With your mamas extension cord
    The kind of nigga calling
    Himself Mister Massa Jones
    The kind of nigga shoving
    His dick down your throat
    To your heart. A polite nigga
    Is nice for dinner,
    But I need a crazy nigga
    For these cookie monster nightmares.

Sacrifice

Always a man sitting
    On the church house steps
    Cruising us unChrist-like
    Legs gapped like the
    Arms of a cross.
    I Pontius Pilate,
    Wash his blood from my lips
    Next Sunday pieces of his
    Skin are offered for communion.

Window Shopping

Ain't in no hurry at all
   Gonna sit in this mall
   Take every bit of it in
   Long as it's tall and thin
   Thin and tall and tall and thin
   Love em all
   niggas niggas niggas!

The Boy Watchers

We sit in secret and in silence
Avoiding each other's eyes
Pretending to eat a fast snack
Pretending to not notice one another.
Eyes sweep over a tall figure in jeans
Sweep from neck to ankle
Hearts beat and wish beat and wish
Like years riding the backs of fluttering butterflies.
Our bellies push against the mall's plastic tables
Our asses fill the cheap seats
Our hearts run over with desire
When he and he walks by us
Like we are rocks in a garden—
Like we once walked by those gazing at us
When we were twenty-two, four, six, and eight
We never dreamed we would turn to rocks
And our only joy, being tickled by plastic ferns
Blowing in air conditioned winds.
Lord here comes a boy now
My red shirt catches his eye
And our eyes meet for a moment
This is my lucky day.
The others curse me under their wheezing breath.

Summer Day
Summer rains come
Catch young men shirtless
Turn black bodies to lacquer.
I taste their sweat
And am reminded of days
Loving in the rose garden,
Daring thorns to pierce my heart.

The Resilient Nigga
Hey nigger, hey nigger
Hey alcoholic nigger, hey nigger
Hey nigger with cut up arms
Hey nigger with your skull in your lap
And the bullet in your eye
Hey nigger whose mama missed you
With the coat hanger and pulled out your sister
Hey nigger, hey nigger, I speak to you
From the black dungeon lit
By my pen. Hey nigger
Hey nigger, hey nigger
Hey crack baby, hey dead daddy's bastard
Hey self-righteous, self-wounded, self-afflicted nigger
Die nigger and go to hell
So I can whisper in your earshell
Songs of hey nigger, hey nigger, hey nigger
All night long.

SMOKE, MIRRORS, AND NIGGAS

The Barbershop oozes smoke mirrors and niggas—
  smoke mirrors and niggas.
  A nigga's cat eye catches mine. He's getting
  An AK47 etched in his head. My tongue travels
  To the valley of death between his legs
  then to his amber eyes.
  If I linger too long in his soul's window,
  will he kiss me or kill me?
  Jeri's Hair Tonic and Wild Root
  Mask the scent of sex between legs.
  Deep voices rumble about the Lakers, Rockets, and
  girl's big asses passing the window.
  Balls bounce between thighs.
  Dusted off and oiled, I pay the price of the ticket and tip
  For the service of human touch.
  The cat eyes occupy a corner
  By the red, white, and blue lamppost.
  "Should I, should I, should I,"
  I ask myself three times
  Before denying brown skin Christ.

Hunting

The woods have been overlaid
    with concrete and crushed red candy
    You part glass doors to enter the oasis
    of Berber carpets and potted plants
    the sun and moon have been pre-empted
    by strips of fluorescent fireflies.
    The animals are still as wild as ever.
    They stand in packs or sometimes alone
    at a water trough transfixed by a melody
    playing in their loins.
    The traps you set are more complex
    than iron teeth with springs
    An old leg of lamb won't do for bait
    In this jungle it takes gold, you have
    to roll Versace and Movado off your buttery tongue.
    A nod toward the Air Jordan store doesn't hurt.
    You wink at one boy who has separated from the herd—on purpose
    He calculates how much bullshit he must dish out
    and how much he must eat.
    "you have very pretty eyes
    I'm reminded of golden almonds…"
    "thank you, sir…"
    'Don't call me sir, Dawg is cool, or Nigga.
    All that respect shit is for ol folks"
    He looks at how you try to disguise four decades of living—
    shaved head, belly straining against the waist of oversized Levy's
    Timberlands snug making your corns cry out. He spies
    the gray nose hair you missed and sighs.
    He opens his script to page three and begins

"I'm so bored. I wish I had someone to talk to
to take me to the movies to help me buy my School clothes..."
On "school" you're hooked. Who doesn't want to help a boy stay in
school?
You pull out your platinum Visa that is almost maximized
to its full potential
But there is still room for Air Jordan's, pizza, and a motel room.
He can't take you home to his Mother younger than you
and you could never explain this to your Rummage Sale wife.
You hold on to the Air Jordan's. You've known them to run off with
the bait
before you can milk them for their nectar
in your dark reserved room number 8 at Motel 6
you don't wait for him to get out of the hard back
chair he has chosen by the black curtains. You lay the bait on the
bed
in the center to be exact. You stand behind him and start to stroke
his neck.
He winces and his belly gurgles, but he can't kill you
After all he was church raised until he turned sixteen and mannish.
so he sighs and hopes that all you want is to get on your knees
and milk him for nectar. He doesn't want to lay his head on your
flabby bosom, kissing is out of the equation.
But hey you want your money's worth. You want him out of those
clothes.
You want him in nothing but Air Jordan's, nothing but Air Jordan's
and dick
It's something about that scene, that image. When did that fetish
hit you?
You close your eyes and block out that Uncle—that one who
Used to make you dress up in your Sunday Shoes and
Nothing else.

Your boy goes along with this game after you've laid out twenty green ones

After all the Air Jordan's will give him back his manhood he thinks. You wash your face and gargle. You both step out into the sunshine his old gray Nike's are left behind in the can. His Thank You is very businesslike, so much so he should be wearing Brooks Brothers instead of jeans sagging.

The rulebook is opened. He doesn't have to recite the canons and codes

You both know them too well.

You drop him 3 blocks away from home,

you turn your head so his posse won't see your face wrinkled like a walnut shell.

Boy in Silver one Summer Day

"Would you like a ride?
    I know you. I've seen you
    bathing in star dust late
    at night on your bed
    and your name is?"

    "Rock. I live down the street, man

    Yes I know you. We live in the
    Same honeycomb building
    And my Mama don't get off
    Her nurse's job 'til midnight.
    We can hang. Do you have videos
    And Captain Crunch?"
"Here we are, Rock
    Push hard on the door
    it hasn't been the same
    since Mama fell dead
    and heavy against its broad back"
    "You're nice. Sorry about
    The milk on the rug,
    But the Knicks, they my boys!
    Cool how you got all their games
    On tape, on tape, Daddy!
    But now I'm bored
    What else you got on tape?
    What's this? Aw, Man!
    Two dudes fucking, fucking
    Like a nigga and a hoe.
    You must be a fag, but that's cool.

You can be one but not me.
And say, cool Daddy, this hay is dope.
My dick is hard. Look at it bouncin'
All by itself. Is your dick hard?"
"As a rock, baby
Come here you soot black
pussy lipped nigga
Don't start giggling like no girl.
You will spoil things like old milk
Take off your Silver suit
Let me kiss your neck for eons."

The silver suit lies on the floor
Shimmering like a patch of sea
At midnight. Rock smiles forever
His babies dry on my thighs
I hear the heavy feet of his mama
Thumping past my door.
She pauses at the dark liquid
Seeping out from the cracks,
lives on to regret that no
Grandchildren will ever rest their
Tired little heads against her bosom.
All she had was Rock

Wonder Boy

Wonder if he has a girl named Kenisha
     if anybody ever whispered boi pussy
     In his caramel ears and does he have
     Phallic dreams of rockets blasting off?
     Wonder if my blues wake him in the night
     As I incant his name,
     Daniel, Daniel, come out of that fire!
     Wonder what's his favorite
     Jack-off trick, wonder if he and other Best Buy boys
     Compare hard drives in dark back rooms?
     Wonder what kind of baby was he
     What kind of man will he be?

Disappointment
the suicidal nigga
danced the jig
on razor blades
soaked in Hennessey
then the doors to
heaven opened
instead of gold avenues
he found cotton fields
even in the land of milk
and honey
you still a field nigga.

21

You strutted into my head
     between my blurred eyes
     as if you owned me and the planets.
     The Rover Explorer crawling Mars
     treads territory you have conquered.
     Your pride puts me on my knees.
     I let you "punish" me for being old.
     Your babies, as big as oysters, slide down my throat.
     My burning cauldron consumes them.
     You collect your drawers from my fists
     pry loose the golden coin from my ass
     There is no evidence you've been in my house
     Except pubic hair I uncurl
     And weave into a shawl.
     Downstairs your eyes catch the reflection
     of future you in the glass door.
     You're ancient and on your knees.
     Your mouth is spread open, your face covered in shimmering jism
     You wonder how you came to this.

Lady Vanity

I like to dress my boys in silky panties
    satin and pink, satin and virgin white as snow,
    satin and red as Satan is evil.
    I like the way the lace fringe rings their hard thighs
    A little T-shirt the kind emblazoned with a
    horned devil holding a pitchfork and the caption
    I'm a little devil is a nice touch especially
    when it rises above the belly button
    winking at the world.
    It's hard to buy panties for boys.
    Even when they have slender hips
    you have to buy a size too large
    to accommodate the stuff. You know, the stuff.
    Sometimes I use old Mrs. Jones to crank them out
    on her ancient foot pedaled Singer.
    More in the crotch. More in the crotch
    I whisper in her ear. Her brow furrows for a moment
    before she shrugs her humped shoulders and follows
    my directive. I go to say something about a girlfriend
    but my voice rises in pitch as the lie scratches my throat.
    I shut my mouth and eyes and dream of Eric prancing
    in all lace. I feel his lips touch mine.
    He is rambunctious and the panties won't stay on for long.
    He'll throw them in my face, pout, and say "I'm no bitch."
    He'll put back on his blowzy boxers, pull his stuff out
    through the crotch and say "C'mon nigga.
    Let's play this game my way."

The Chocolate Eater

I love you so much,"
   Said the blonde-whiskered devil
   To the boy in blue spandex, black skin, and curls.
   "I love you, I love you so much,
   I'll eat you with my teeth.
   I'll eat deep into your black decay
   Until I become you. This is
   My love's goal, baby,
   To become you. I can't stand
   Myself in my mirror. I must
   Love you—Love you until
   I'm so full, only your sex
   Hangs from my lips. Yes!"

SCAT

The boy mashes your brown turds
Feeling for the glittery glass sprinkles
He's cooked up in the greenish meatloaf
And you thought
He was being kinky—
He adds more slivers
From your Mama's old mirror
Until your shit runs crimson.

The DL

He's cute and quiet
   Chin and cheekbone
   make a point
   Of an isosceles triangle
   Legs gapped and
   Mouth closed
   He takes this man-thing
   Like a man
   I dig into the brown earth
   Dig and dig until I reach
   His serenity
   At that moment
   He opens his mouth
   And coos softly
   Thanks, man, thanks.

Windows

I like open windows—
Their wide-eyed dreams.
I like them high, away from prying eyes
But low enough for him walking by to see.
I like being fucked in front
Of open windows,
Like showing my business
To sparrows, flies, and God.
Sometimes when there is no man
I lie in the window anyway and wink
My brown eye at the chameleon
Turning translucent on the clear glass—
—his red heart beating like a fly's wing.

CAR SEX

The Mustang
Two young men ride a slope back mustang
Sit wide legged as
Buckets hug their ass in soft leather and they
Stroke the dickshift between them.
The driver glanced at me. Eyes lit up
Like headlamps. He remembered my face
in a dream. In a dream
he wore his Mother's mink stole and nothing else
as he sat on my sofa with legs lifted up
and I blew his dick.
My sharp teeth woke him
He sprang up in bed, clutched his crotch, massaged
His hard dick, got into his rhythm, shot some blanks
Fell back to sleep, forgot the dream
Until he spied me in the red Corolla (which means crown)
Then it all came back to him.
He told his boy,
"I dreamed that fag sucked my dick."

From A 3rd Floor Window

At first
When the red coup
Showed up
He'd sit in
The passenger side
Legs wide
Pulling the hem
Of his shorts
To his knees in manly modesty.
They shared a forty-ounce
Hands gripping the neck of the bottle
As if it was a cock.
Back and forth, back and forth
Thick lips shared this communion.
Now
The shirts are chest-high
Shorts slip to crotch
Fingers interlock
Like rivets.
"Take eat of this flesh," the radio drones.
As the foam
Drips from their yearning tongues.

Dude in a Red Car

There goes that dude
In the dorky car, cute
He is, all curls and sweet bell face.
The car red and rolling
Body bent like a crab
Reminds me of a baby's shoe.
A rainbow colored YMCA
Sticker is plastered across the hood
Like a child's bandaged forehead.
I pull along beside him—
Traffic is jammed east
And west on Snake Road
So we sit paused and pondering.
As the sun smothers his face.
I give him my best orthodontic crafted smile.
He looks at me for a second.
In that interlude where neurons
Seek reason and recognition,
I was someone
He thought he knew from the Y.
Then he saw me clearer. My intentions
Glittering off my teeth and blazing out of my eye-sockets.
He saw my gaping mouth cave.
That looks like the glory hole
In an adult bookstore toilet.
He snarled an insult at me
Gunned his motor
While I wished I was the road
He was rolling over.

Testosterone

Three jeeps in a row
    Man-driven, one with a Bull Mastiff
    Riding shotgun, tongue
    Large and wet like a pink salmon.
    Then came the Datsun 280Z roaring up the rear.
    Where was all of that man juice going?
    Were these Jonathans racing to meet their Davids?
    Woof! Barked the Bull Mastiff
    At the red Corolla winking and tipping his tiara.

HISTORY

Antique Roadshow

Topsy's feather duster Value $150,000—
    She used it to dust all over the plantation house
    Even used it to beat a mouse.
    She plucked them feathers from a peacock herself,
    Feathers of gold, blue, and emerald.
    She was gonna make herself a hat.
    But Missus said a feather duster would be more useful,
    And that was that.
    When Topsy turned antique,
    They sold her for a buck fifty.
    Poor Topsy, not even worth the price
    Of her own feather duster.

History 2257

Let the nigga
   rise up horselike
   on hind legs.
   Let it beat drums
   Wail 1000 years of blues.
   Let it be
   Let it see
   Into the future
   Metropolis of burning cities.
   Let the nigga burn
   And unburn
   Let the nigga write
   History in the year 2257 AD
   It's coming—
   Cloned niggas
   Cloned whites
   The KKK and the Panther cloning itself
   And titanium crosses and iron fists
   Being nuclear bombed to orange
   In the future days.
   Let the nigga be running
   Let the nigga be writing
   Letters from a Soledad prison.
   Let the nigga think it's new
   Until a white man digs out
   The old parchment
   Buried in Angela Davis' heart.
   Aint nothing new under the burning sun
   What Pharaoh did

We still do.
What the dinosaur did
We die too and come back
As purple sap to burn lamplights
And launch bullets.
Let the nigga be slaved and not slaved
               (There was a nigga President when?
                    Haw! Haw! Haw!
                You lie like a son of a bitch
               Never been no such thang.)
Let the nigga who is
Your great great great great
Grandson's grandson deny us
As he sits in a bar built over your bones
Drinking plutonium cocktails
But when a white man researches our history,
Let the nigga open his eyes
And demand reciprocity and equality in the history books
Once again. Once again.

The Revolution
Eleven years old and bird legged when all that stuff
was happening. All that stuff—revolutionary Black Power stuff
all that Panther stuff
H Rap, Stokely Carmichael, Angela Davis stuff
That stuff that made us strut our stuff
My Mama didn't let my hair puff
But we strutted our stuff on MLK Boulevard
Formerly known as South Park
She bought that house there
On Okinawa Street...
Remegan, Mountbatten Eisenhower Dunkirk Doolittle Pershing
All around our stuff...World War II street names
Where white folks relived history.
My mama and me did our stuff in the middle of "nigger"
And dog sic'ing's, we did our stuff—
An enigmatic light skin negro woman widowed
And a slender black boy orphaned
In that house she had painted yella.
That was not a cowardly act
It was her being herself
Her act of bravery in 1966
And not just us, but a sprinkle of us,
A dot of pepper here and a dot of pepper there
In that sea of salt
Right in the middle of that South Park Houston Texas stuff.

Gentrification—The Future of Third Ward and Wards Everywhere

They sure have built this up.
Used to be a slum full of homes
Tin roofed homes that beat a rat a tat tat in the rain.
A shack to you, a home to me.
A shack to you, a home to me.
Eight lived there and in the summer
Aired their funk on the front porch while drinking Jax
Used to be so black—even at noon even at noon,
Jitterbug black Marcus Garvey black
Black panther black, Elijah Mohammed black
Used to so black Third Ward black
Dowling Street Black Ten Ten Live Oak Black
Jack's Cab black, Forward Times black
Fairchild's Funeral Home black, Delano Street black
Wheeler Street black, KYOK and KCOH Black
Used to be liquor store black, Scott Street black
Still Frenchy's Black, Still Cuney Homes black, Emancipation Park
Black,
But it used to be so black, Hotsie Totsie and Daddy Deeeeep
Throat Black
I said Daddy Deeeeep Throat Black, A mountain of soul black
Miss Emma and Daddy MacMurray Black
Gertrude, Doris, Savannah and Clarence Harvey Black, Tom the
Jap's Fish market Black
I said it used to be so black—
Before there **was** Wholefoods, Starbucks, Target, Crave Cupcakes
And the condo people who crave cupcakes and ten-dollar coffee
A choo choo train and a stadium where they kick balls.
Gone are the shotgun houses, blood stains, the bullet holes
Gone are the Church's that didn't become museum pieces

Left is the cemetery that irritates the Condo dwellers
We wail loud when we come to bury somebody anybody
We wail loud and sing over the patio fences
We wail loud with our mouths black as graves
We wail so loud they run to cocaine and valium
To drown our voices.
They sure have built this up.
Used to be a slum full of homes
Tin roofed homes that beat a rat a tat tat in the rain.
A shack to you, a home to me.
A shack to you, a home to me.
So I sit here by my shopping cart reading
Ebony from 1970,
While they pass by and by waltzing to trendy cafés.
Ain't no law against being a monument
I remind them and the police.
Over and over again.

The Ghetto is the World

"The world is a ghetto."
    Remember when they used to say that?
    Now the ghetto is the world
    We walk by on the corner of
    Main and Despair.
    There is still an afroed boy running amuck
    In the muck of shit and piss
    The seventies forgot him
    Ronald Reagan forgot him
    The Bush wars forgot him
    The slums let him slide
    But these people here
    They done closed up the projects
    Done bought up the land
    Gave him a job at McBurger's
    He can eat at cost
    But he can't sleep anywhere anymore
    But at the corner of
    Main and Despair.
    Becky jogs by
    With tits a flopping to the rhythm
    Of her ponytail and ass.
    He is free to look.
    No more Emmett Till moments in Money
    But if he had money, he could buy Becky
    If he had Becky, he would have everything that is nothing
    Including a hut behind a picket fence
    And a chariot chained to the finance company,
    But there is no American dream chained

To the corner of Main and Despair.

Dealey Plaza 2015
Sirens wail like women
And motorcycles gun their throats.
A President's skull cracks open
Like an exploding egg.
Black cars speed by like panthers
Blood paints the sparrows red
Cardinals wail and moan
Leaves shimmer and shine.
A whale spits out Oswald
He has one deadly eye
Walks up to me
And points at the speck of him
In my dark pupils.
"I am innocent," he says
A man named Ruby walks past
Holding thirty pieces of silver.
He tosses them into the air
Oswald call tails
"Tails is death," Ruby says
"Last coin seals your fate."
The Kennedy Half Dollar blocks the sun
Bounces off a cloud, wobbles
Like it's wounded
Before landing face down.
Ruby pulls six triggers
And moves on, but takes a moment
To look at Oswald's ass.

Decency
When they shot ol' Bowser
They did have the decency
To kick him to see if he still breathed,
Did have the decency
To grab him by the tail
Drag him to the side of the road,
To lie in a patch of blue bonnets and buttercups.
They did so much less for, and not in any particular order—
Tamir Rice, Michael Brown, Trayvon Martin, Eric Harris
Walter Scott, Phillip White, Freddie Gray, Tony Robinson,
Tamir Rice, did I say Tamir Rice? I'll say it again, Tamir Rice,
And it won't be the last time we'll be breathing names in poems
Like wind going through trees.
A kick to the heart might have
Jumpstarted the blood beating
A hand over wounds might have kept blood in the vessel
Might have silenced a mother's crying.
But they didn't want their butchery on their hands.
Oh those Pontius Pilates,
Just a kick might have shown
They had some decency.

Go Bang! Bang!
guns bang bang america the beautiful
blood runs from chicago to the big easy.
to get a gun in bang bang america
gun crazy fingers finger coin triggers.
not niggers, but white folks
galore and glory in being lone wolf
in batman clothing, angels in trench coats
toting assault rifles and licking sperm soaked fingers.
men are buckshot crazy. The NRA goosesteps
into kindergartens, apples on the end of bayonets
pointing at teachers to teach a convoluted constitutional
amendment. I don't want seconds to live. I want millenniums.
Mums on my grave for being brave enough
to go to the mall, movies, or mortuary.
Here me be lying in my coffin all dead
soft cotton stuffed in holes in my head
singing...
"guns bang bang america the beautiful"
through teeth spit out by lead.

A BAD BOY

The Rebellion
Sometimes I want to
stand in front of movie screens
step on some pretty toes
grab some crotches, goose an ass
laugh at funerals
cause eyes to fall upon me
as if I'm in a room of startled cats.
I don't care about disapproving
Head shakes, mouths flapping open.
I get tired of obeying the rules.
Why can't I wear a dress to the office,
And my nice birthday suit to a wedding?
It fits me better than anything I ever bought at Brooks
Brothers.
Yeah, I wear white in December
Greet the Fed-Ex guy in pink lace panties
Why not use the women's bathroom
Especially, if you have to shit?
Shitting and sitting is as good there as anywhere.
Why is the world so alarmed by the FUCK YOU in
fuscia
On the trunk of my caddy and the ox head
Riding the hood?
I painted my house lime green.
The hurricane's eye saw it well and left it alone.
It beat the neighbor's beige box to splinterings.

I want an elephant for a fucking pet—house broken though
  Imagine Ol' Lady Jones popping her eyes out
  At Dumbo taking a shit in her petunias—on a leash
  All the arrests I've endured
  for poking holes in the theory of man's freedom.
  I wrote that Obama man and told him
  To paint the White House jet black
  But leave the front door red—
  Red as a virgin's puss...
  Okay, vagina
  There. I followed a rule. I was nice.

To know not one
My mother used to tell me
I needed a good strong man to beat my ass
Beat it to know not one
I did not know forty years later
I would crave such a beast
That I would look at thick black belts
Wrapped around stout bellies and waists
And yearn to be stripped
And brought to my knees
To have welts spell my name
And mark my sins.
At eight such a possibility frightened me
At twelve it drove me to sniff gas
From the Chamber's range
At forty, I ogle the braided and studded beasts
Holding tight trousers to thick bellies.
I imagine buckles looped over hammy fists
I hear the song the leather sings
And feel the flesh it cracks.

Tamed

Would I have survived without the foot on my neck?
What if I had been unfettered unbridled
What if wild was let run wild?
Who would have been my killers?
Man, woman, disease or a triptych of all three?
"You need a man to beat the living shit out of you,"
My mother said standing on my neck.
She conjured up that man
From the grave of her first husband—Jesse Ficklin.
Everyday, everyday instead of the blues,
I beat the shit out of myself while
Strangling my neck in chokeholds
To keep myself in check against my wild self

Farting at Funerals and in The Museum of Lies

Do not fart in the African-American section
    Of mask wearing spear chuckers.
    Do not fart there.
    Go to the room of oiled portraits
    Of buxom ladies, of cock sucking gents.
    Go where the Madonna and child repose so peacefully
    Upon downy clouds and, sapphire skies, and golden suns—
    Go there to stink up the joint
    With your day old collards, beans, onions, and yams.
    Fart until the room steams and empties itself
    Of offended sensibilities.
    Fart at grandma's funeral
    As her pinched face swallows the formaldehyde
    Offend Aunt Sarah and her Aunt too.
    Offend, Offend, Offend.
    What other weapons do you have, quiet one?
    I am a good man, a decent man.
    I go to church
    And jack off to Jesus
    Hanging on that cross
    After being buggered by
    By Roman cocks.
    Lord, why have you left me?
    Deacons have not been trained for my unholy dance
    Museum guards have not studied quiet rebellions.
    My voice is muted as oil on canvases.
    But here come the authorities, tongues caught in throats,
    White imps come to deal with a black devil.

The shit I couldn't figure out where to put, so I guess it's the end of the book

A Blank Canvas

The canvas is blank.
What colors should I be today?
I'm not seeing red, not singing the blues.
Are shades of gray, Lady Ambivalence's hues?
Sundays, I wears a sherbet shawl
Of orange, lime, and green.
If I want to, I sport summer in the fall
Leaves turn yellow before they die
So why can't orange accompany
The widow to the grave?
Not too crazy about beige, putty, or mud.
Ought to be a law against such dull duds.
Perhaps this is a white day.
"All my days ease on by
Green and yellow,"
Said the sky.
"But it's not summer yet," I said.
"Don't matter," he answered.
"Now is the time for your shroud.
There is no time to question rainbows
Stitching hems in the sky."

Six Cents

The words from the spirits
    are worth six cents thus sayeth Scribd.
    A lifetime of blood and eyeballing ... six cents
    finger cramps and tears ... six cents
    the blues blowing through my head ... six cents
    The 3AM walks around the bed ... six cents
    Well it's a little better than
    A penny for your thoughts.

Gatesville Texas

"For more years or four more queers?"
  Johnny guffawed and hee hawed louder than ten Satans
  His belly shook like punch in blue bib overalls.
  He wore a gingham hanky around his neck and
  Resembled a chicken who met the axe.
  "Johnny's just a big silly bowl of pudding,"
  his mother said slicing am apple pie
  with a serrated butcher's knife.
  In the yard a car leaned sideways
  On wheels and bricks
  A flagpole waved the stars and bars.
  Obama hung in effigy from a poplar tree.
  At dusk the sun bowed to the moon
  Blackbirds tucked head under wing
  Johnny spat his last wad of snuff
  Into the gardenias.
  He stepped past his mama snoozing
  In front of *Let's Make A Deal*—
  Waddled to his room
  Clicked on his computer
  And stripped in blue light
  As images of naked black boys
  Filled the screen and danced in his glass
  Of Old Grand Dad.
  Then Johnny fell to his knees and prayed all night
  He prayed until his mouth watered
  Prayed until his sperm dried and cracked on his knuckles.

The Edge of Madness
It started with a pink cowboy hat
And a pink baton he used
To poke at women who turned
Their disinterested heads.
The black pants rose high
Over his ankles and shined
In the ass like dull glass.
The coat was blue corduroy
Even in the summer
Even in the rain.
Then the lights were disconnected
And he burned the land lady's cat
In the fireplace so he could write
And he offered her the bones
But she was not having that
Nor his poems that went
Something like Plath
Itch itch itch itch
And the moon became his
Night companion on the nights
It felt like shining.
He threw a brick at a horses ass
But missed and dismounted a cop
In jail he lectured the iron bars
Until a deputy's fist knocked
His teeth all over the psych unit.
They let him go, pink hat and funky
Clothes. They kept the brick.
He wanders now and wonders
Why the stars are on fire.
He listens to the lamppost.

It tells him when he's hungry and
When it's time to shit, sometimes
Right then and there on Main in the middle
Of the lunch crowd who try to avoid
His nature
And wonder what shit drove him crazy?

The Black Sea

I absorbed her subtle lies
    When she uttered
    "Soot black tar baby
    Can't see nothing but his teeth
    Nigger so black he scares himself"
    All of this from a black woman
    High yellow and running from
    The Black Sea rising up.

Money
The store the farm the river the fan—
The perfect square of life lived and unlived.
It took Money to steal a smile unjustly.
What would Caroline
Do today if she still had Money in her blood?
Would she confess her love for Emmett's song?
What would Emmett do if he could turn
A square inside out, a frown upside down?

My Jonah

Man in that water
    Churning away in that
    Dirty wash water.
    Wife looking for him
    Can't find him.
    Beach patrol in the sky
    Flying a one eyed bird
    Looking for that dude
    Can't find him
    God told Saint Peter
    To go down and fetch him
    The saint went to the water
    Looked all over for his soul
    Reported back to God,
    "Can't find him."
    Water churned over
    And said, "I got him.
    I got a whale to feed
    Going to make him my Jonah.
    I said I got a whale to feed.
    Going to make him my Jonah."

New York THOTs

4 corners of black women
Madison Ave and 49th squared
Black, blue, orange, and pink
Blouses billowing.
Cat eyes meet at the shoes
Sandals, flats, heels, wedges
Checking and judging THOT—
"THOT, who she think she is?"
The light turns green with envy
A bus rumbles by—
My THOTs disappear.

The Girl in the Salmon Blouse
A fish eye over each nipple,
Gleaming silver winking at me.
Salmon are ready to lay eggs
In her fertile valley.
Their gills have beat her breast bloody
Her cart is loaded with wine,
And a case of Budweiser.
All sorrow will be drowned tonight—
All sorrow washed away with
Bloody eggs, wine, beer, and sperm.

Cities

They're gritty loud nasty
Like your old big mama
They'll knock your ass off
And help you get up.
A burnt offering might
Yield you some candy or
Some whole lot of trouble.
Know when to speak and
When to speak back
Know when to look
And when to look back
Know when to love
And know when to keep your eyes
Focused on the trash rolling
Down the sidewalk.

He Has the Most

His body in summertime—
   Sticky maple syrup
   Poured over smoked skin and bones.
   Not a stitch on
   Except shorts the color of old motor oil.
   He wanders through parking lots
   And people, trying
   To catch up with his life
   Pacing a few steps ahead.
   Where is his bed, I wonder?
   Alone in mine I ponder.
   The dumpster feeds him well,
   But his blood burns it up
   Leaving only lean stories matted in his hair.

Purple Secrets

I got secrets
We all got secrets
But I got secrets
Deep as graves.
Walgreen's got no cure
For the purple blues that ails me,
For the purple rain that drowns me.

The Lamp #2
The lamp across the way
Lime green like sick grass
Never lights but spies
With open eyes
Peering night and day from
Between red curtains
And resting upon
A frail chest.
She mocks my days and doom
With laughter
Behind her tattered shade.
"I am dark and soon will be your days."

Flatline
I want to write newspapers
Not ten line epistles.
We're young until we die,
Always foolish
Until our hearts skip
A final beat
Flatliiiiiiiiinnnnnnneeeee
But before that
True love is always fresh after a storm
The world is round for a reason
Don't walk into corners
Lest you become history.

How to tell who the old men are

Get close sniff for pungent Icy Hot Patches,
    Run the metal detector over them
    Listen for pacemaker's song,
    The hip beating cymbals with metal bones.
    Look under their tongues for the bitter garlic
    Check their cloudy eyes for cynicism
    Brush your hand across their spongy cocks
    Steal their bank statements
    Check off all of the doctor's visits and trips
    To the pharmacologist
    Sneak their mail
    And read the reports from their proctologist
    "Your prostate is the size of a fist."
    Mark the tires on their cars
    See how they never move
    Watch them sneaking into Club Boyland
    Baseball caps low over their eyes
    Stumbling through the miasma with cataracts.
    Listen to their stories and wonder
    What the hell is a rotary phone and
    How did RI7-0866 connect with the outside world?
    Check their mouths for receding gums
    And removable teeth..
    Check the hem of their pants for low hanging balls.
    Check, check, check, everything
    And then check your own expiration date.

That Boy
He's watching from behind his owl-eyed glasses
Because he's curious.
He's heard things about you
From his daddy the cop,
From his grandmother the sullen non-speaker.
They've warned him to stay away from you – *that man*
Pointed at the parts of his body, they said
You would snatch from him.
"If he says a word to you, run!"
But last night he had a dream about you
In the dream he did not run, could not run
Stood like a pillar of salt under the moon
As you crawled towards him
And the wind from your mouth
disturbed his red basketball shorts.
In the daylight as they pass – daddy cop and sullen grandmother
You note he's almost as tall as his father
All three wear glasses, making them look like owls.
His eyes linger a moment in your face
As he remembers the dream and warm breath
Tickling him until the dawn turned purple.

Two More Seconds of Joy
There were certain things he believed
Perhaps rather foolishly—hard work will make you rich,
Childhood ass whippings made him a good man—but
One thing he believed fervently was
That an old man should always
Have a younger man in the house.
A fresh talisman to ward off
The grim reaper.
There was no tonic, or mashed vegetables
More potent than youth, he swore.
To prove his theory,
He watched his ride-or-die friends—
All ten of them die alone
In their homes of soft sofas and chairs
Die alone in their Queen Ann beds
Die alone as their Mercedes sat in garages cooling heels.
He didn't die, didn't even get old, as he heaved his body
Over tombstones and fresh graves,
While the Grim Reaper visited Restful Pines
And picked withered fruit.
Some pals had been whores in their day
Some had been saints
But they died while he grew younger
And had a young man to watch.
He held onto his theory
On his birthday he sang,
Just another day, the Lord has kept me
Grateful not to the Lord in Heaven
But to the Lord in Sponge Bob drawers
Making pancakes in his kitchen.

When there was no one else
To watch die and die alone
And just before the nurse closed his eyes,
He wondered if his theory had been foolish
But he glimpsed through the IV lines into the lighted hall
A Mohawk, muscle-shirt, and a pair of tight red pants switching side to side,
And received two more seconds of joy.

Little Sister

He called upon his mother to rise
From the grave, but there was
No earthly body, only bones
And threads of a gold evening gown
Tossed across the breastbone.
A diamond ear stud glittered in her skull.
In the pelvic bones lie fragments of fish bones.
The mortician shrugged.
"There is no sea near here,
And you said your mother hated seafood.
This is a mysterious mystery."
But the coroner put his eyes on the bones
And declared them tiny fingers and toes.
"They stayed in the womb.
The rest of us aren't so lucky."
So he named his little sister Lucky
And took her home in a jar.
For the next thirty years, he told her stories
About the woman who carried her
To heaven and beyond.

<u>Vegas</u>

All we did was sit in vast Harrah's
Stuff ourselves with buffets
And lose lots of loot.
We weren't good road dogs
We should have suggested
Things like—I don't know
Anything involving testosterone
And other fellas
One of us would have struck luck
I'm sure
All we did was lose
And walk to Target in the rain.

The <u>**Artist**</u>

After his book signing
    He jumped out his fourteenth floor window
    And went to pieces all over the cobblestones
    of 666 Main Street.
    The devil made him do it.
    God did not stop him
     for he was an **"artist"** and tormented.
    His prickly heart picked up
    subtle insults—handshakes too slight,
    smiles that faded too quickly,
    eyes that did not linger, and tongues
    that refused
     to caress his ego—for he was an **"artist"**.
    To cure himself, he propped opened the door
    Of his hotel room with his old *Webster's*,
    started from the brocaded hall,
    Sprinted across the maroon
    blood colored rug,
    Crashed though the glass
    as if it was made of sugar
    And for twenty-nine seconds he was fucking happy.

The Mirror

Framed in faux wood
The color of cockroaches
Surrounds the ocean of gray glass dreams
Where eyes swim like minnows
Bearing witness to the whore on the bed
The suicide hanging bt the neck
A cock sawing an ass
And the ugly suitcase
Spilling its guts.
Never a dull moment
For the mirror.

Sister Brown Had the Last Word

We do our dead wrong
Pumping them with chemicals
And wiring their jaws shut.
Let them speak!
They see God sitting at the
Right hand of the devil.
The dead know the truth.
They know why Laura Mae cursed on
Saturday and sang on Sunday.
They know there ain't no
Streets paved in gold.
But that lamb's got some balls
Biting the lion's tail clean off at the butt
And making him eat it.
The devil don't use no pitchfork either.
He got a big thang like you saw
In the adult novelty store.
The saints are tortured, the sinners are saved.
George Wallace and Bull Connor is up there
Sucking the black boys they beat.
Mother Theresa didn't quite make it.
Her sins were too great from when she was a child.
God can be an ironic bitch.
The dead see all and know more than they see.
They'd tell us, but Smalls wires their jaws shut tight
And glues their eyelids so they can't blink
One for yes, two for no.
We got the dead all shut up
In gilded satin lined boxes
To bury in a cold hole close to hell.
Burning them would be better

I'd rather wail at black smoke
Ashes and bits of singed hair
Floating toward Heaven.
Fire is more majestic than dirt clods
Going thunk thunk on a tin lid.

Now it ain't no formaldehyde in Sister Brown
Because you can't mix embalming fluid with alcohol.
They found her dead and the flies
Buzzing drunkenly into each other as if they were blind.
And Smalls old hearse caught fire
Just as they loaded her in.
Sister Brown's ashes inherited the earth she never owned.

Untitled

Hang on that tree nigger
    Hang on that tree
    Hang on that tree nigger
    Hang on that tree
    Hang on that tree nigger man
    Hang on that tree
    White man got your nuts
    In his hand
    Hang on that tree nigger man
    Hang on that tree.
    Hang on that tree nigger
    Hang on that tree
    Hang on that tree nigger man
    Hang on that tree
    White man cut off your right hand
    Oh nigger man hang on that tree
    Hang on that tree
    Oh nigger man hang on that tree.
    Hang on that tree nigger
    Hang on that tree
    Hang on that tree nigger
    Hang on that tree
    White man gouge your eyes out
    Hang on that tree
    White man gouge your eyes out
    Nigger hang on that tree
    White man gouge your eyes out
    Oh nigger hang on that tree
    What's coming next, you can't see

Hang on that tree nigger
Nigger hang on that tree
Hang on that tree nigger
Hang on that tree
Hang on that tree nigger man
Hang on that tree.
White man got your nuts in his hand
Hang on that tree nigger man
Hang on that tree
Hang on that tree nigger
Hang on that tree
Whoa, nigger hang on that tree
Hang on that tree
White man cut your ears off nigger
Hang on that tree
I say white man cut your ears off, nigger
Hang on that tree
Can't hear yourself scream nigger
Oh can't hear yourself scream
Hang on that tree, nigger
Hang on that tree
Hang on that tree nigger
Hang on that tree
White man cut your foot off, nigger
Whoa, hang on that tree
Got your foot running nigger
Oh got your foot running
I say white man got your feet running nigger
Oh nigger watch your feet running
Hang on that tree nigger
Hang on that tree
Hang on that tree nigger

Hang on that tree
Whoa nigger hang on that tree.
Hang on that tree nigger
Hang on that tree
Hang on that tree nigger
Oh hang on that tree
Heah come the fire nigger
Dancing like Daniel
Oh heah come the fire dancing like Shadrach
Oh heah come the fire nigger
Dancing like mashack and Abegnego
Oh heah come the fire nigger
But you can't get back
Hang on that tree nigger
Hang on that tree
I say Hang on that tree nigger
Hang on that tree
White man got your tongue nigger
Oh you can't shout
White man got your tongue nigger
You can't holler and shout
White man cut your nose off nigger
And leave you a snout
Oh white man cut your nose off nigger
Can't smell that kerosene
Hang on that tree nigger
Can't smell your flesh a roasting
Hang on that tree nigger
Hang on that tree
God done gorgot you nigger
Hang on that tree
I said God done forgot you nigger

Hang on that tree.
Army coat wrapped around you nigger
But Uncle Sam can't save you nigger
Oh hang on that tree nigger
Hang on that tree
American flag pole stuck in tour ass nigger
But hang on that tree
Jesse Owens running and Joe Louis boxing
But hang on that tree nigger
Hang on that tree
Martin Luther King dreaming
But hang on that tree
Obama soon coming nigger
But hang on that tree.
Hang on that tree nigger
Oh Lord, hang on that tree.

About the Author

Charles W. Harvey is a native Houstonian and a graduate of the University of Houston. Charles was a 1st place prize recipient of PEN/Discovery for Cheeseburger, which went on to be published in the Ontario Review. Harvey was also awarded the Cultural Arts Council of Houston Grant for Writers and Artists. Charles has been published in Soulfires, Story Magazine SHADE, High Infidelity, The James White Review, and recently NEWVERSENEWS. He is the author of the novels The Butterfly Killer, The Road to Astroworld, and Antoine's Double Trouble. He is also the author of several stories and poetry collections.

Connect with Harvey

Don't miss out!

Visit the website below and you can sign up to receive emails whenever Charles Harvey publishes a new book. There's no charge and no obligation.

https://books2read.com/r/B-A-EWG-RJDS

BOOKS 2 READ

Connecting independent readers to independent writers.

About the Author

Charles W. Harvey is a native Houstonian and a graduate of the University of Houston. At UofH he studied fiction under the guidance of Rosellen Brown and Chitra Divakaruni. In 1987, Charles was a 1st place prize recipient of PEN/Discovery for his short story Cheeseburger, which went on to be published in the Ontario Review. In 1989 Charles Harvey was awarded the Cultural Arts Council of Houston Grant for Writers and Artists. Also in 1989 he was a finalist in the MacDonald's Literary Achievement Awards. Charles has been published in Soulfires, Story Magazine SHADE, High Infidelity, The James White Review, and others. He is the author of the novels The Butterfly Killer, The Road to Astroworld, and Antoine's Double Trouble. He is also the author of several story and poetry collections. He also writes for the stage and screen.

Read more at https://charlesharveyauthor.wordpress.com.

About the Publisher

Wes Writers and Publishers strives to bring you great books for your reading pleasure. We have been in the business of producing quality works of fiction for over two decades. We will branch out in the future to add more authors to bring you the reader, very high quality and entertaining stories from all genres. It begins with Charles W. Harvey our star prize winning literary writer an poet. He is the author of the prize winning short story Cheeseburger selected by Joyce Carol Oates in the 1987 PEN/Southwest Prize. He is a frequent participant in NANOWRIMO and other literary endeavors. Please feel free to sample his many stories and two Novels via Smashwords and other fine retailers. AC Adams brings you a little something different. He is our premier author for the gay literary erotica genre. Many of our readers have enjoyed his Roommates series. Look forward for a lot more to come from this up and coming author. Clarissa Haley comes from east Texas. She likes quirky little stories that swim around that brain of hers. She has several exciting projects in the works. She has a few romance stories in the works for future release Wes Writers and Publishers (we like being called WWP) will be adding more l writers under its wings in the near future. We love good stories.

Read more at https://charlesharveyauthor.wordpress.com.